How to Sparkle at

PREDICTION SKILLS

Jo Laurence

Brilliant Publications

We hope you and your class enjoy using this book. Other books in the series include:

English titles
How to Sparkle at Writing Stories and Poems   1 897675 18 6
How to Sparkle at Phonics   1 897675 14 3
How to Sparkle at Nursery Rhymes   1 897675 16 X
How to Sparkle at Grammar and Punctuation   1 897675 19 4
How to Sparkle at Alphabet Skills   1 897675 17 8

Maths titles
How to Sparkle at Number Bonds   1 897675 34 8
How to Sparkle at Counting to 10   1 897675 27 5
How to Sparkle at Addition and Subtraction to 20   1 897675 28 3
How to Sparkle at Beginning Multiplication and Division   1 897675 30 5

Science titles
How to Sparkle at Assessing Science   1 897675 20 8
How to Sparkle at Science Investigations   1 897675 36 4

If you would like further information on these or other titles published by Brilliant Publications, please write to the address given below.

Published by Brilliant Publications, The Old School Yard, Leighton Road, Northall, Dunstable, Bedfordshire LU6 2HA

Written by Jo Laurence
Illustrated by Kate Ford

Printed in Malta by Interprint Ltd

© Jo Laurence 1996
ISBN 1 897675 15 1

First published 1996
Reprinted 2000
10 9 8 7 6 5 4 3 2

The right of Jo Laurence to be identified as author of this work has been asserted by her in accordance with the Copyright, Designs and Patents Act 1988.

Contents

Introduction

This book is one of a set of four devoted to basic strategies which will help early or beginning readers to find their way through the maze of complicated skills which make up the ability to read.

All the activities in this book are to do with prediction skills and word recognition. They are designed to teach children to predict and anticipate which words come next, through their awareness of context and syntax, and to build up a basic sight vocabulary of words which they will meet often.

It is a fact that a few, perhaps 100, words form a foundation for all texts, particularly those offered to young children.

By encouraging early readers to perceive those words either from context or from recognition of words in their bank of sight vocabulary, we help them to develop an understanding of the relationship of written words to spoken language and also to read with more speed. This is crucial for fluency and for confidence-building.

Because many common or high-frequency words are not phonically regular in their spelling pattern, children often have difficulty in breaking down and blending their sounds. This can result in confusion because words that do not fit their perceptions can make a nonsense of all the phonic rules they have already absorbed.

Often it is impossible either to illustrate or explain the common words. A word such as 'was' for instance, or 'that', can only take its meaning from the words that surround it. It is not easy to explain these words to a child. The speed with which a child can either recognise the word or anticipate its being in the sentence will add to the fluency and accuracy of his/her reading ability.

The other three books in this series deal with the alphabet and alphabetical order, phonics and the development of sequencing and comprehension skills.

How to use this book

The activity pages in this book are designed to supplement your chosen reading material.

They can be used with individual children or with small groups, as the need arises. They have been written in such a way that the text is kept as short as possible so that early readers will feel confident to tackle them without too much teacher input. On the other hand, some children may require you to read through the page carefully with them before they embark upon the activities.

The order in which the pages is arranged is not particularly the order in which children should tackle them. Rather they should be used randomly as and when reinforcement is required or the need for development of a particular skill is recognised.

It is not the author's intention that a teacher should expect all children to complete all the sheets, and especially not in any particular period of time. A flexible approach and a knowledge of the sheets and of the children's needs will provide the teacher with a bank of work that will enable children to extend their knowledge and understanding of the reading process and thus their mastery of it.

Some of the sheets can be used in different ways. For example, pages 47 and 48 can be used as follows:

- To play Bingo have groups of four children. Divide a copy of the sheet into three equal sections and give them to three of the children together with some counters or a pencil to cross words off. The fourth child will be the caller and he/she needs a cut-up sheet of words put into a bag or a box. The caller takes out a word at random and reads it out. When a child finds the word on the sheet it is covered or crossed out. The first player to fill his/her sheet wins. The players can then swap cards.

- Play Word Snap. The children play in pairs. Each child needs a set of the words. The words are separated and the children deal them as with an ordinary game of snap. If the words match they call snap. The first to call wins the pair. They keep going over and over the words until they are all paired. The child with the most pairs at the end wins.

- Play Word Pairs. You need two sets of the words. The words are separated and are placed face-down on the floor or a table. The children take turns to turn over any two cards. A child who turns two that match keeps the pair and has another go. The winner is the one with most pairs when all the words are exhausted.

- Separate the words. Give a child the words you are trying to teach. Have the child choose a book from the book corner and look for the words on the cards. How many times can they find the words in their book?

The word sheets would, of course, have a longer life if they were stuck to card before they were cut up.

Links to the National Curriculum

This book fits in with the National Curriculum Programme of Study for Key Stage 1 Reading attainment by offering practice in the acquisition of:

2   Key Skills

a   They should be taught to use various approaches to word identification and recognition, and to use their understanding of grammatical structure and the meaning of the text as a whole to make sense of print.

b   Word recognition, focusing on the development of a vocabulary of words recognised and understood automatically and quickly. This should extend from a few words of personal importance to a large number of words from books and the environment. Pupils should be shown how to use their sight vocabulary to help them read words that have similar features. They should discuss alternative meanings of words and phrases.

Grammatical knowledge, focusing on the way language is ordered and organised into sentences (syntax). Pupils should be shown how to use their knowledge of word order and the structure of written language to confirm or check meaning. Pupils should be taught to recognise the value of surrounding text in identifying unknown words.

Contextual understanding, focusing on meaning dervied from the text as a whole. In order to confirm the sense of what they read, pupils should be taught to use their knowledge of book conventions, story structure, patterns of language and presentational devices, and their background knowledge and understanding of the content of a book. They should be taught to keep the overall sense of a passage in mind as a checking device.

Extension ideas

The following activities will develop word recognition and context prediction skills in order to broaden the children's use of language and add to their reading ability.

- Concentrate on showing words which have real meaning to the children, such as names of friends or pets and labels in the classroom/environment.

- Rather than teach isolated words, give some contextual clues to their meanings. For example, write a sentence with the key word highlighted. Read out the sentence, pointing to each word, and have the children join in at the highlighted word.

- Cut up the sentence cards and ask children to 'find' the different words for you so that you can make up the sentence together.

- Write blackboard stories together. As you write the sentences that the children have composed on the board (ask them to read along with you), stop and ask 'What word do you think should come next?' For example, if you have written:

The boy was running ...

   the children could offer *down*, *along*, *around*, *into* amongst other words. For each offering ask them to tell you what they think might come after their suggestion. Lead them to see how their choice of word will change the sentence/context. Decide together what your final sentence should be.

- Make up games for:
  *   matching words to pictures
  *   matching written words to spoken pictures
  *   matching written words to written words
  *   matching and guessing words from initial letters and picture/descriptions

- Cut out a set of large shapes and a set of small shapes. Choose high-frequency words that you want the children to learn. Print a chosen word large on a large shape and small on a small shape. The children play in pairs. Lay all the large shapes, word facing upwards, on the floor. One child chooses a word from the small shapes randomly and the other child has to jump or hop onto the large shape with the same word.

- Let the children choose and cut pictures from mail-order catalogues. They stick the pictures to small cards. Each child gives you a phrase or sentence to fit their picture. You print it carefully on a strip of card in front of the child, pointing out each word. Help the children to learn the words. The children can share their picture cards and word strips. In groups of three or four, they could mix the cards up and then match the right word strips to the picture cards. You can develop this by making the groups larger, by giving the whole set of cards to pairs of children, and eventually by cutting the word strips into sections so that the children have to anticipate, recognise and match the words and the pictures.

Name the pictures

Choose from the words.

It is a _____.
fin
fish
ship

It is a _____.
shine
chop
shoe

It is a _____.
spider
spot
side

It is a _____.
black
balloon
bone

It is a _____.
key
kitten
kite

It is a _____.
cool
clock
cook

Make up two of your own:

It is a _____.

_____

_____

It is a _____.

_____

_____

Colour the star if
you can find the
word 'kitten' on
this page.

Picture words

Circle the picture name.

(door)	doll door dear	(star)	stay star stick
(ball)	bath ball bell	(apple)	any ample apple
(tree)	tree train tape	(girl skipping)	skate sick skip
(cake)	came cake click	(mouse)	moon money mouse

Do two pictures and words of your own.

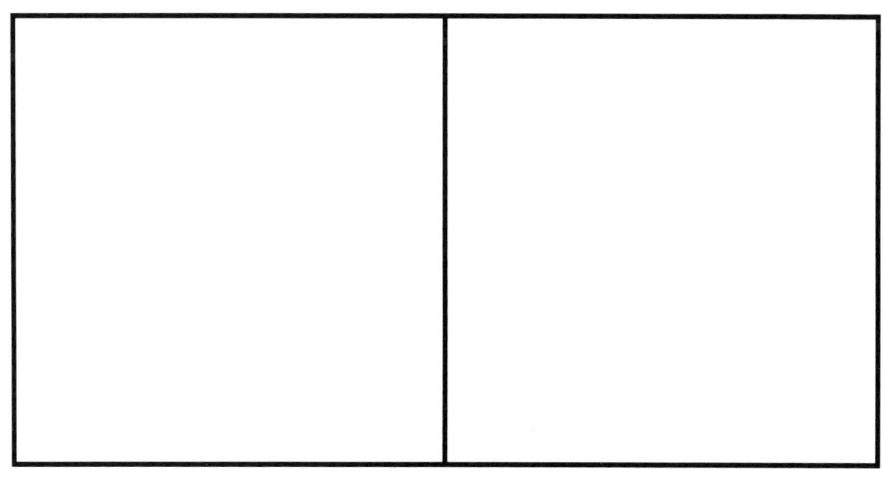

Colour the star if you
can find the word
'train' on this page.

Match the size

Draw a circle round the right one.

little

middle sized

big

small

middle sized

large

Write the size words here:

Colour the star if you can tell the story of the three pigs.

Do you know these words?

Write the word which fits each sentence.

up   to   round   over   in   on

Jack and Jill went _____ the hill.

Here we go _____ the mulberry bush.

The bear goes _____ the mountain.

Ding dong bell, the pussy is _____ the well.

Ride a cock horse _____ Banbury Cross.

Humpty Dumpty sat _____ the wall.

Colour the star if you can say all the rhymes.

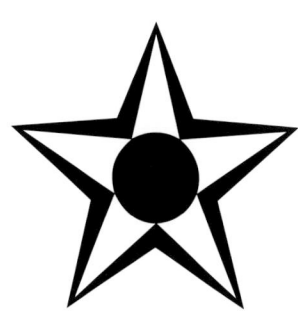

Number words

Write the word for each number.

1 _ _ _

2 _ _ _

3 _ _ _ _ _

4 _ _ _ _

5 _ _ _ _

6 _ _ _

7 _ _ _ _ _

8 _ _ _ _ _

9 _ _ _ _

10 _ _ _

Which one is a flower?

a cup
butter
a buttercup

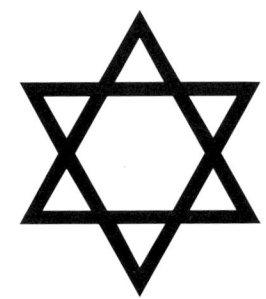

**Colour the star
if you can
name another
flower.**

Finish the words

Write the letters from each cloud to finish the words.

b _ _ _

c _ _ _

f _ _ _

h _ _ _

w _ _ _

d _ _

g _ _

h _ _

n _ _

p _ _

c _ _ _

f _ _ _

g _ _ _

h _ _ _

t _ _ _

b _ _

g _ _

l _ _

m _ _

w _ _

at

b _ _

c _ _

f _ _

h _ _

m _ _

Colour the star if you can read
all the words.

Cats and mice

cat	This is a cat.
mouse	This is a mouse.

Match the words:

cat   mouse

mouse   cat

cats	These are cats.
mice	These are mice.

Match the words:

cats   mice

mice   cats

Match the words:

cat   mice

mice   cat

mouse   cats

cats   mouse

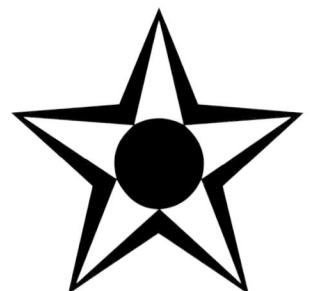

Trace the words:

Colour the star if you can
count all the cats and mice
in the pictures.

What is missing?

Fill in the missing words.

The three bears

Once there were three bears. Mummy Bear, Daddy Bear and

Baby Bear. They _____ ____ __ _____ ____ _____

_____. Every morning they had _____ _____

_____.

One day they went for a walk, instead of eating their porridge.

Someone _____ ____ _____ _____. Her name

_____ _____. When the bears came back,

Goldilocks was _____ _____ ____ _____

_____ _____.

- -

was Goldilocks

porridge for breakfast

lived in a cottage in the woods

came to the cottage

fast asleep in Baby Bear's bed.

Colour the star if you can tell the whole story.

What makes sense?

Circle the word that makes the most sense in each space.

One day / month a flying cup / saucer landed in Ranjit's garden / house

Ranjit rushed outside to sea / see what was happy / happening

Out of the space ship / boat stepped an alien. The alien was green / ground

with four eyes / pies . It waggled its ants / antennae at Ranjit and scared / said

'Are you the leader? Can / Calm you hope / help me?'

Write what happened next.

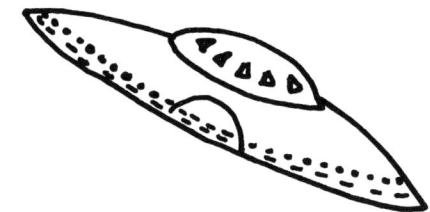

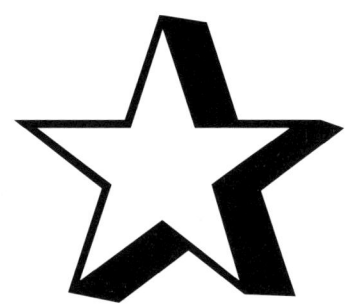

Colour the star if you
can draw Ranjit and
the alien.

Cut and stick

Cut out a  .   Stick it here.

Write the word _____

Cut out a  .   Stick it here.

Write the word _____

Cut out a  .   Stick it here.

Write the word _____

Cut out a   Stick it here.

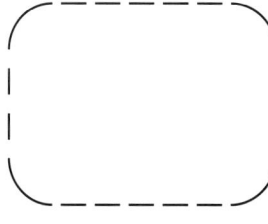

Write the word _____

Colour the star if you can find the word 'stick' five times on this page.

tree butterfly house flower

Cut

Cut and stick shapes

Cut out a ▲ .

Stick it here.

Write the word _____

Cut out a ● .

Stick it here.

Write the word _____

Cut out a ■ .

Stick it here.

Write the word _____

Cut out a ◆ .

Stick it here.

Write the word _____

Colour the star if you can read the words.

diamond   circle   square   triangle

Cut

Same sound, different meaning

Circle the word that names each picture.

I eye		be bee	
eight ate	**8**	to two	**2**
flower flour		tale tail	
sun son		buoy boy	

Can you finish these pairs of words that sound the same? Write them here.

pair ?	red ?
meat ?	blue ?

Colour the star if you can think of any more pairs.

The

How many different ways can you write 'the'?

Here are three to start you off: the the the

Try yours here:

Find different ways of writing:

a	it

to	I

Colour the star if you can write
each word in six different ways.

Words in words

Circle the word that contains the smaller word.

tea teacher lesson	**lay** park playground	**in** lunch dinner
read reading writing	**in** outside window	**draw** cupboard drawing
air balloon chair	**bed** sleeping bedroom	**sun** sunflower summer

Find a big word that contains these little words.

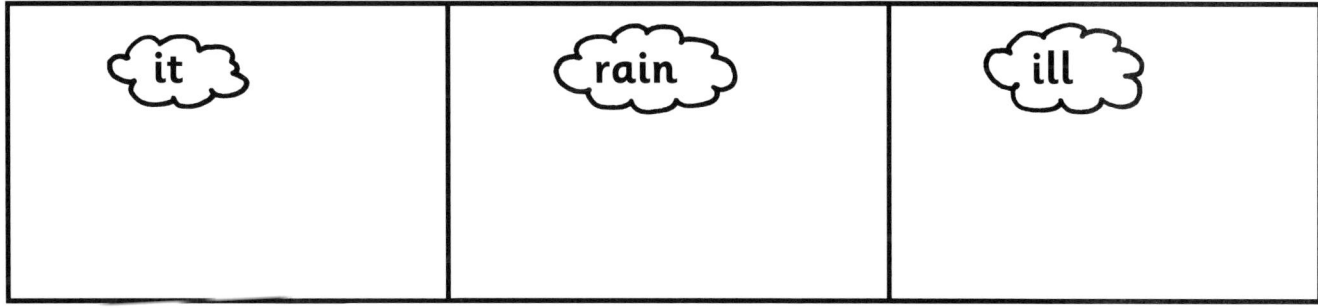

it	**rain**	**ill**

Colour the star if you know a
word that has 'pit' in it and a
word that has 'pat' in it.
Clue: rain does it!

At the supermarket

Choose the right words.

We are all _____ bringing / shopping . The trolley is nearly

_____ full / empty . The lady sits at the _____ chair / check-out

to add up all the _____ things / prices . We pack the shopping

into _____ boxes / packet . When it's loaded into the car

_____ bag / boot we will all go _____ home / fast .

Colour the star if you can read and write the word 'supermarket'.

Spot the odd one out

Read the words carefully. Circle the odd word out in each line.

off	off	off	of	off
saw	saw	was	saw	saw
and	end	and	and	and
by	be	by	by	by
me	me	me	my	me
be	be	be	be	by
if	if	of	if	if
we	us	we	we	we
on	no	on	on	on
as	as	an	as	as
an	in	in	in	in
us	us	is	us	us

Colour the star if you can read all the words.

Find two

Read the words carefully. Circle the words that match in each line.

come	came	cone	come	can
down	drown	brown	down	doom
jest	just	just	jewel	jeer
fist	first	fir	first	friend
more	money	merry	many	more
seat	sea	seen	seen	some
them	their	they	their	think
much	must	mist	much	most
look	like	lot	like	little
home	here	hurt	him	here

How many pairs of words can you find?

Colour the star if you can read all the words.

Find the right sentence

Read the sentences and look at the pictures.
Draw a line from the picture to the right sentence.

There's a pig in a pen.
There's a pig on a plane.

There's a bear at the door.
There's a bear in the car.

There's a bee on my nose.
There's a bee on my hat.

There's a cat in my pocket.
There's a cat in a basket.

There's a duck in the tree.
There's a duck on the pond.

There's a dog on my skates.
There's a dog in a kennel.

Do three of your own.

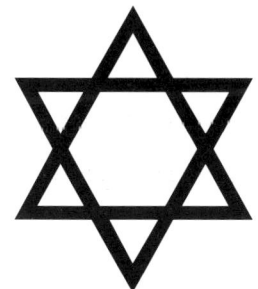

Colour the star if there is a bear in a car on this page.

Swap words

Read the words carefully. Write another word that means the same in the empty box. Draw a picture to go with it.

Use these words:

friends

insect

bicycle

mum

father

Do one of your own here.

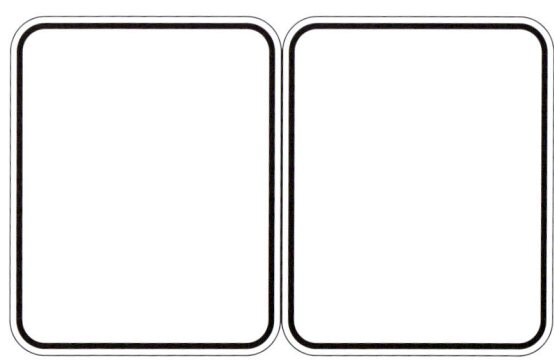

Colour the star if you can think of two more.

Staircases

Fill in the staircases. Use each word only once.

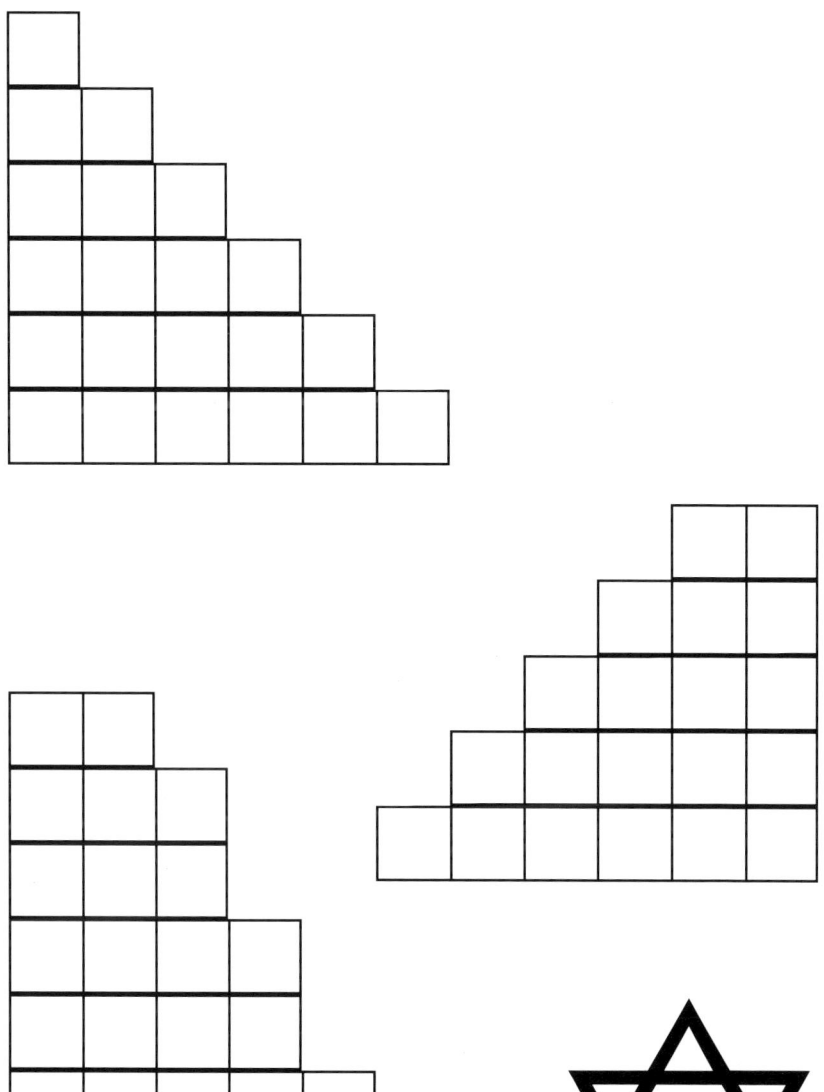

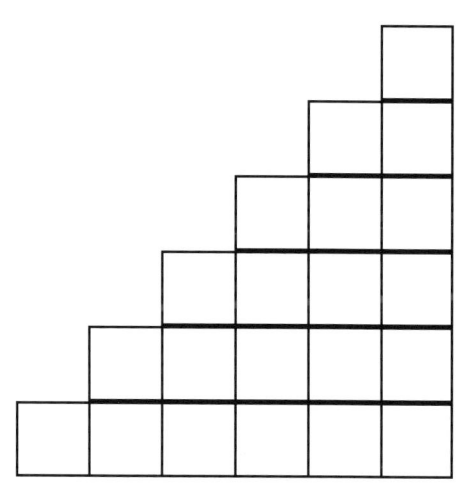

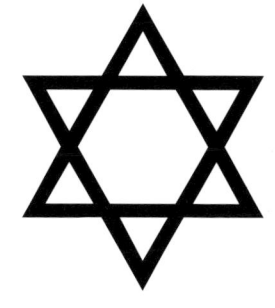

Colour the star if you can fill this staircase with your own words.

Use these words

little	them	I
about	him	am
the	but	have
said	and	from
there	by	a
to	that	could
before	an	where
she	school	

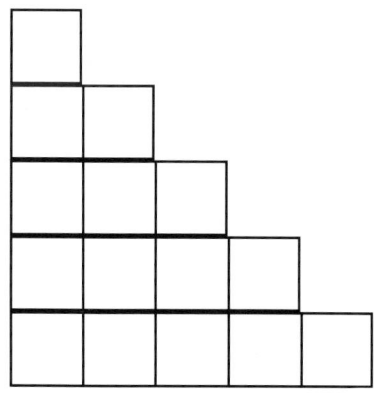

Find the words

**Some words keep coming into a story over and over again.
Read this story and circle the words.**

Once there was a dragon called Donna. The dragon lived in a town

by a school. Every day Donna watched the children go to school and

wished she could go too. When the children played in the playground

the dragon was sad. She wished she was a little girl instead of a

dragon so that she could skip with the children. But she wasn't a girl.

She was a big, frightening creature

and she couldn't skip. A tear ran

down her face.

How many did you find?

the [ ] was [ ] a [ ]

**Colour the star if you can
write or tell what
happened next.**

What comes next?

Continue the pictures on the storyboard.

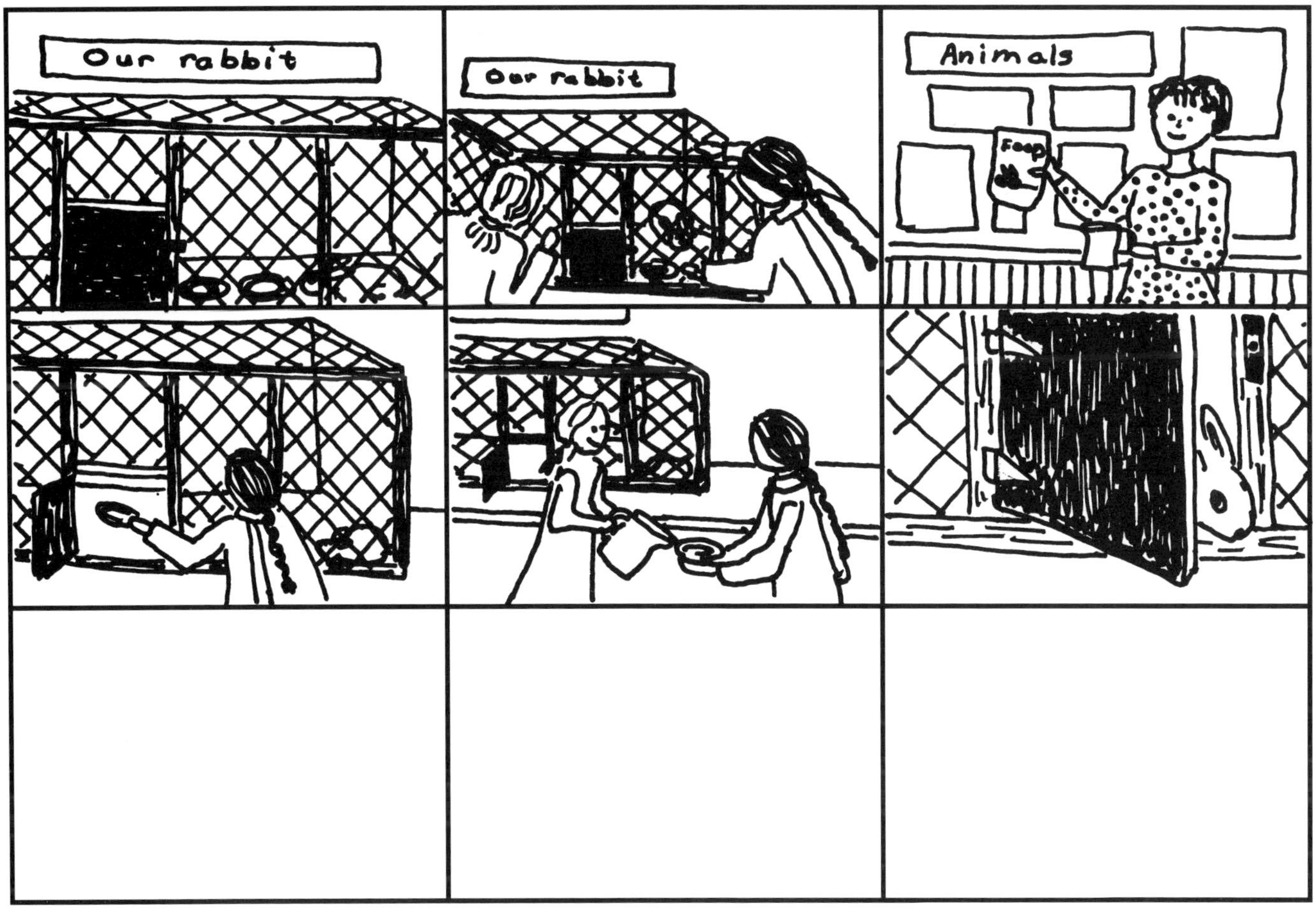

Our rabbit
Our rabbit
Animals
Food

Write the story here.

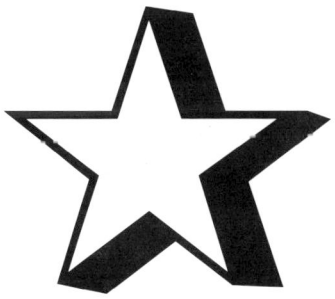

Colour the star if you can read your story to a friend.

Questions, questions

Use these words to fill in the spaces. Read them first.

who   when   why   what   which   where   how

	is your birthday?
	many cards will you have?
	will send them?
	will you put the cards?
	will they send them to you?
	cards will you keep?
	will you choose for a present?

Colour the star if you can answer all the questions here.

Make new words

Use 's' to make new words.

bird + s   =

toy +   =

pet +   =

chatter +   =

Use 'ing' to make new words.

sing + ing   =

wish +   =

play +   =

read +   =

Use 'ed' to make new words.

play + ed   =

jump +   =

paint +   =

walk +   =

Colour the star if you can make three new words from 'sing'.

Fun in the park

What can you do in the park?
Match the pictures with the words.

play on the swings

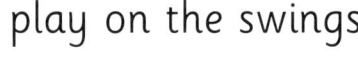

feed the ducks

ride on a bus

go on the slide

climb on the climbing frame

Write which one you can't do in the park:

Colour the star if you can say three more things you can do at the park.

Find the clues

Look at the picture.

Fill in the spaces in the story by looking for clues.

The children are at _____ _____. The _____ is taking

_____ _____ for a _____. The _____ is _____

his _____. They don't know an _____ is hiding round

_____ _____. The alien might look scary, but he only

_____ to play. Will he be able to sit on the _____ or

the roundabout? Will he _____ the children?

Use these words:

bike   girl   park   corner   boy   walk   alien

wants   her   the   frighten   the   riding   dog   swings

Write what happens next.

Colour the star if you can draw an alien.

Riddle-me-ree

Solve these riddles.

It has big eyes
It jumps.
It's green.
It's a _____ .

It is made of plastic.
It has four wheels.
It has a steering wheel.
It's a toy _____ .

It has two wheels.
It has pedals.
I ride it.
It's my _____ .

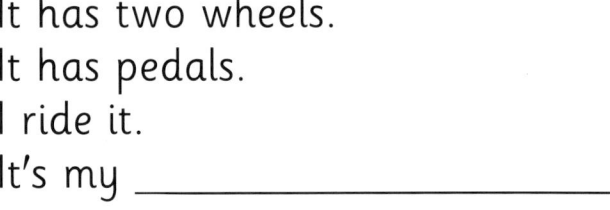

It's made of paper.
It has a cover.
It has pictures.
It's a _____ .

It has four paws.
It has a furry tail.
It likes milk.
It is a _____ .

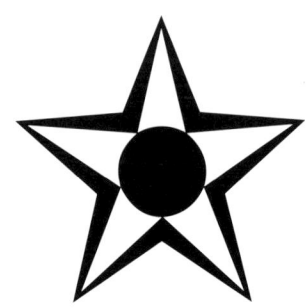

Make up your own riddle here:

It _____

It _____

It _____

It _____

**Colour the star if you can draw a
clue for your own riddle.**

Choose another word

Read each sentence. Look at the word that is underlined. Circle the word that means the same.

The <u>little</u> kitten plays.

   small   fun   black

The teacher is very <u>kind</u>.

   cross   jolly   nice

Jack is a <u>happy</u> boy.

   naughty   cheerful   angry

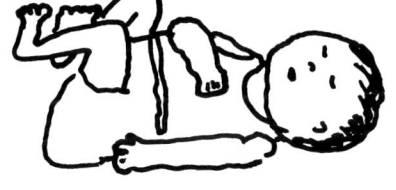

The baby is <u>tired</u>.

   sleepy   good   hungry

Dad <u>fixed</u> the car.

   drove   mended   cleaned

Write the new sentences here.

Colour the star if you can make
a new sentence of your own.

Pairs

Join the pairs that are the same.

Join the pairs that are opposites.

first   little
happy   in
big   last
out   sad

day   right
cold   up
wrong   night
down   hot

soft   bad
wet   dry
under   over
good   hard

Can you finish the pairs of opposites?

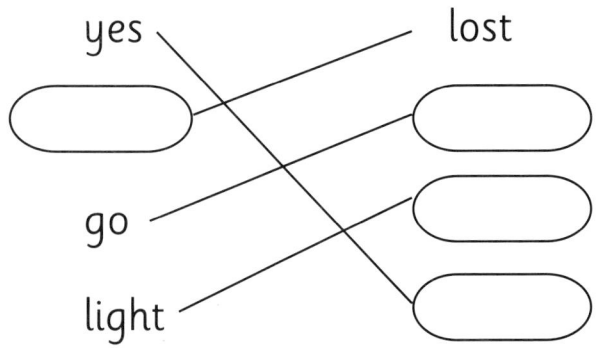

yes   lost

go

light

Colour the star if you can think of three more pairs of opposites.

Building bricks

Colour the building bricks.

blue for numbers

red for people

green for animals

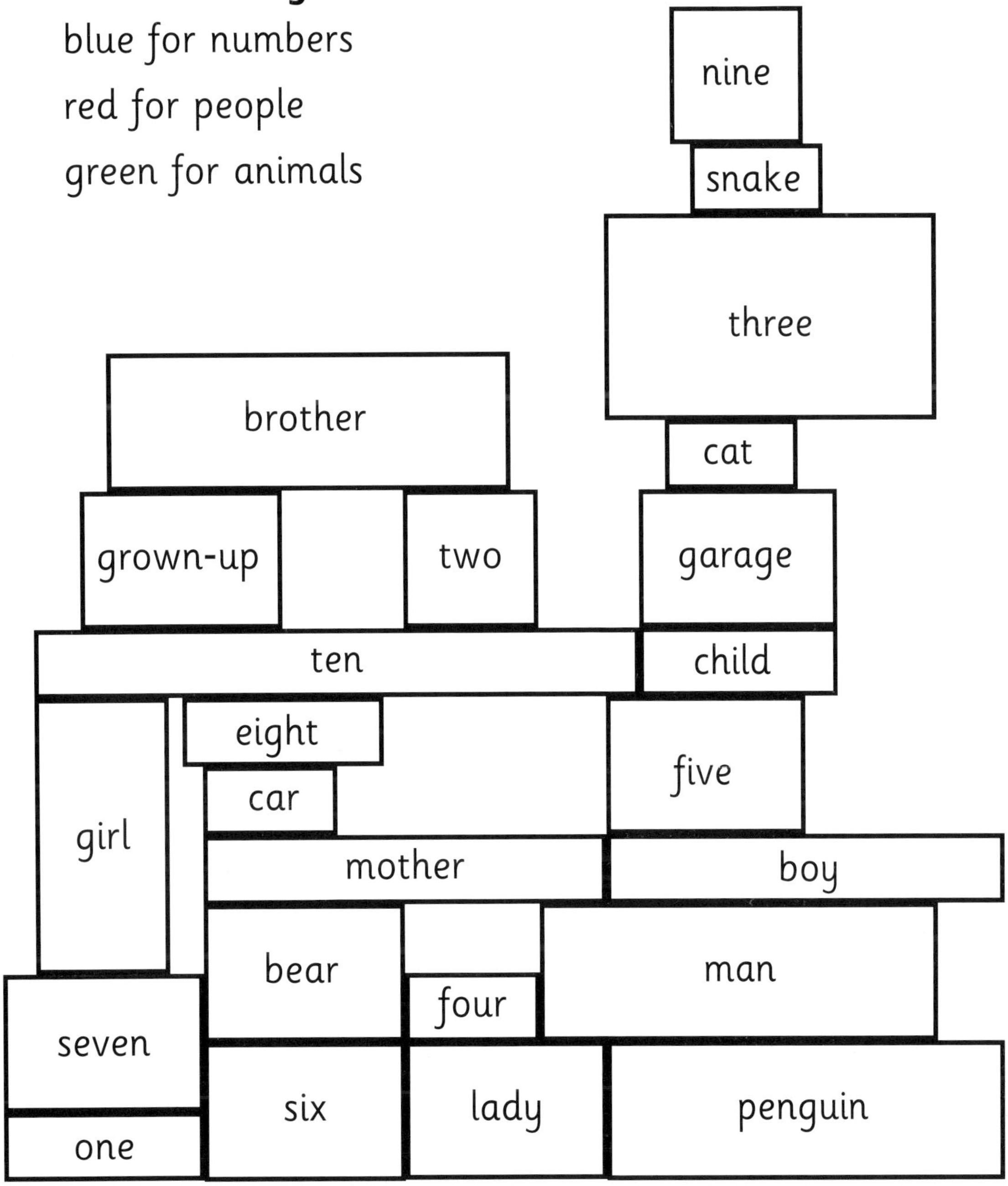

nine

snake

three

cat

brother

| grown-up | | two |

garage

| ten | child |

eight

car

five

girl

| mother | boy |

bear

four

man

seven

| six | lady | penguin |

one

Have you coloured in every brick?

How many are left?

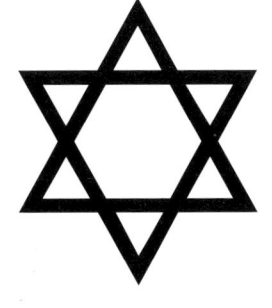

Colour the star if you can read the words that aren't coloured in.

What can you do?

Finish the sentences. Choose from these words.

run skate jump eat build read
swim sing skip paint climb count

I can_____. I can_____. I can_____.

I can_____. I can_____. I can_____.

I can_____.

How many words are left over?

Colour the star if you can draw two of the spare words and write the sentences.

Guess which word

Things that work in pairs are often easy to guess even if you can't read the word.

Can you guess these? Use the clues around the page to help you.

moon

fork

comb

white

woman

black and _ _ _ _ _ _

cat and _ _ _ _

knife and _ _ _ _ _

man and _ _ _ _ _ _

hat and _ _ _ _ _ _

eggs and _ _ _ _ _ _

bread and _ _ _ _ _ _ _

brush and _ _ _ _ _

thunder and _ _ _ _ _ _ _ _ _

sun and _ _ _ _ _

football

dog

scarf

bacon

butter

lightning

There is one word too many.

Which one is it?

Colour the star if you can think of two more pairs.

Match the words

Match the words to make sentences.

She was   the birthday party.

Dad had made   birthday.

The children all   six today.

It was Becky's   birthday card from Gran.

There was a   a cake with candles.

Her friends came for   sang 'Happy Birthday to You!'.

**Put the sentences in the right order.
Write the story here.**

**Colour the star if
you can draw a
picture of the story.**

Word portrait

This page is to fill in a word portrait of you. It should tell:

- what you are called
- how old you are
- where you live

- who you play with
- what you like to play
- what you like best in school

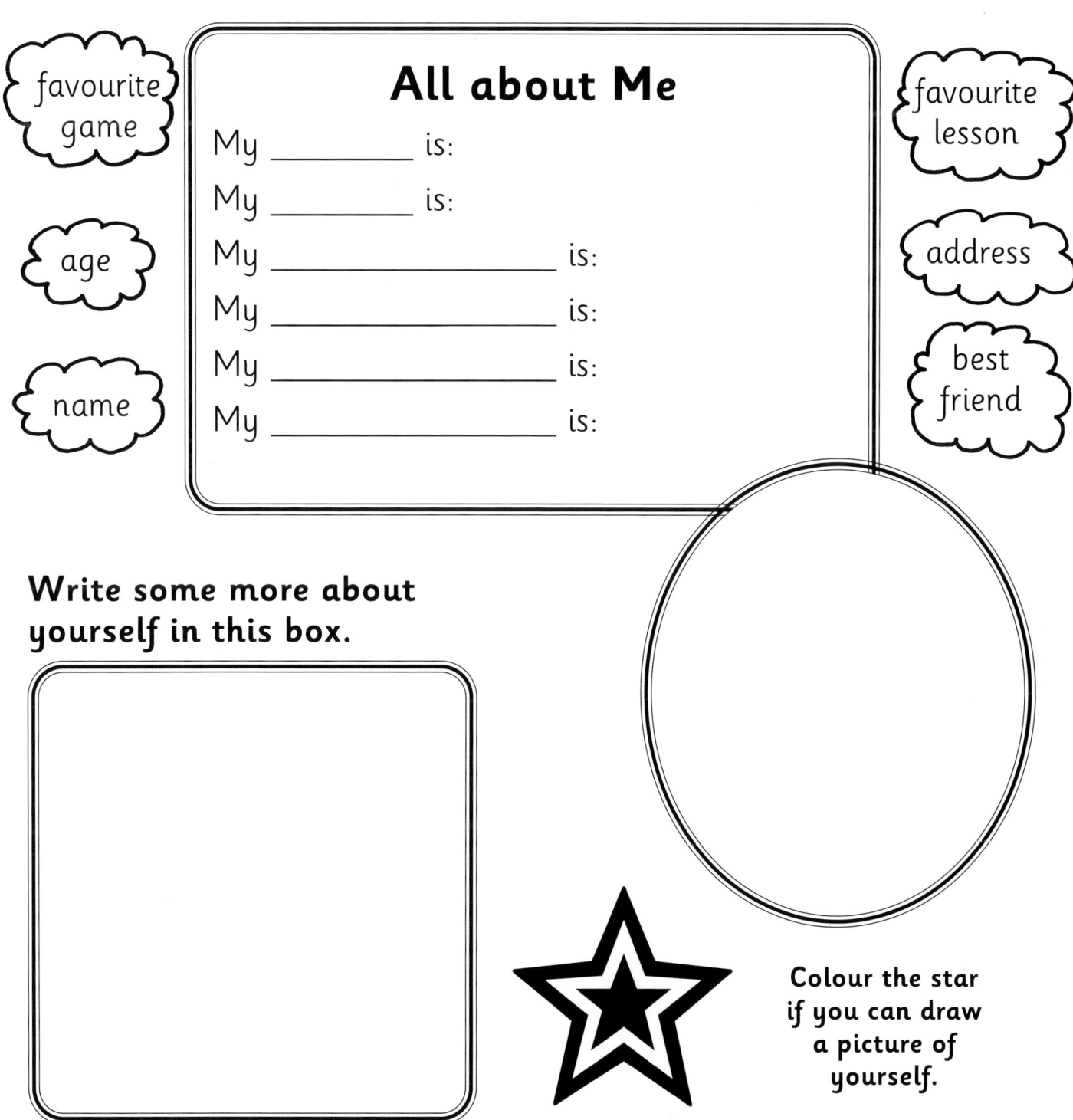

favourite game

age

name

All about Me

My _____ is:

My _____ is:

My _____ is:

My _____ is:

My _____ is:

My _____ is:

favourite lesson

address

best friend

Write some more about yourself in this box.

Colour the star if you can draw a picture of yourself.

Word search

Can you find these family words?

dad, uncle, brother, gran, aunt, mum, cousin, baby, grandad, sister

g	r	a	n	d	a	d	s
r	m	z	y	a	q	x	i
a	u	n	t	d	f	e	s
n	m	u	n	c	l	e	t
m	b	a	b	y	s	t	e
f	r	i	e	n	d	j	r
w	n	c	o	u	s	i	n
b	r	o	t	h	e	r	q

Colour the star if you
can find the word
'friend'.

Sort the words

The days of the week have all got muddled up.
Can you sort them out?

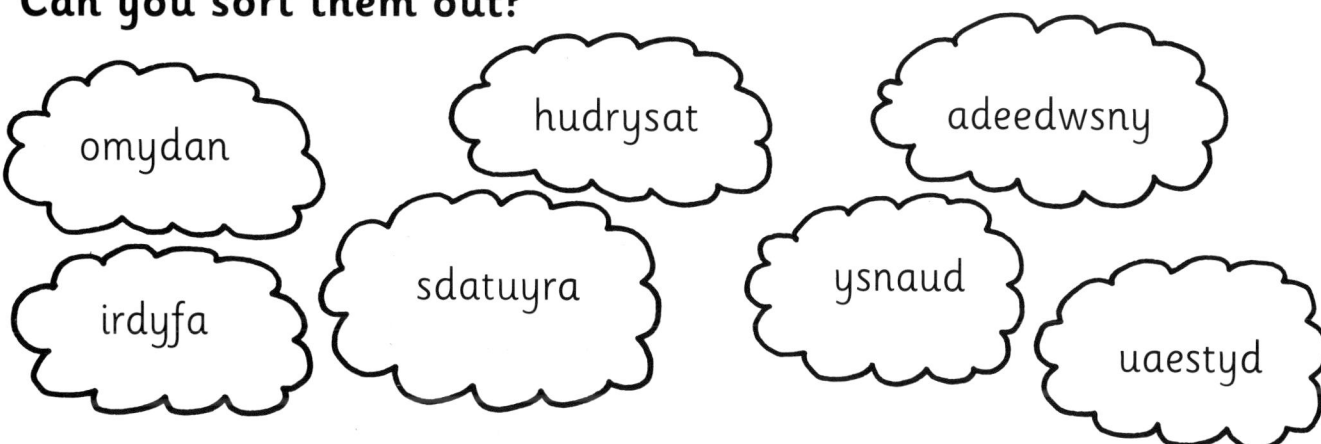

omydan

hudrysat

adeedwsny

irdyfa

sdatuyra

ysnaud

uaestyd

Now try sorting out the months of the year.

yjlu

byufrear

yma

chamr

uugsat

neuj

aunjyar

crobtoe

esbrepmte

rlipa

erbovnem

bceeemdr

Colour the star if you can say
the days and the months in
the right order.

Picture puzzle

Write each picture name in the puzzle.

Across

1

2

5

6

Down

1

3

4

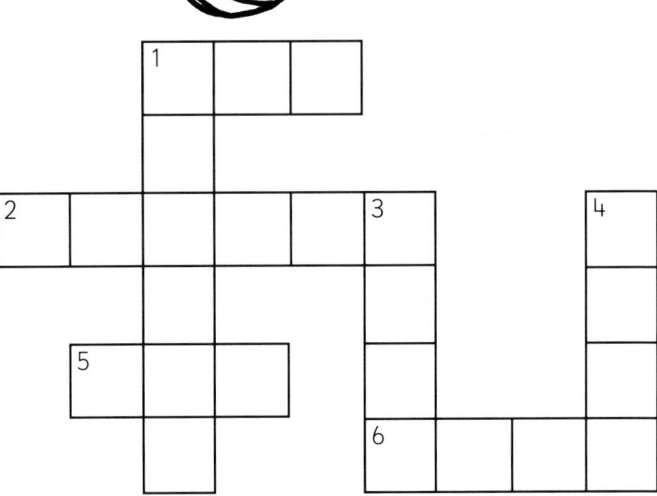

Can you make a puzzle to fit this grid?

Across

1

3

Down

2

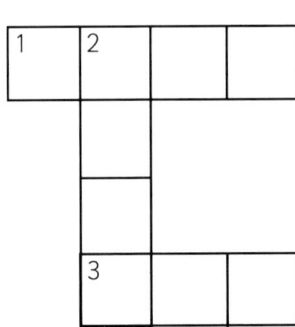

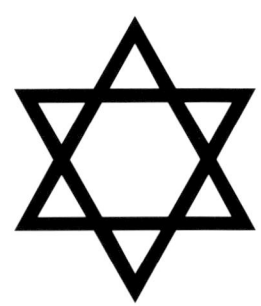

Colour the star
if you have
made a puzzle
of your own.

Picture puzzle story

Solve the puzzle.

Across

2

4

5

Down

1

3

Write a story using the words.

Colour the star if
you can draw a
picture to go with
your story.

Animal puzzle

Do you know these creatures?

1 This one swims

2 This one grunts

3 This one flies

4 This one has a long neck

5 This one likes mud

6 This one has stripes

7 This one is playful

8 This one is king of the jungle

		i					
		i					
		i					
		i					
		i					
		i					
		i					
		i					

Write clues for these.

	m	o	u	s	e	
	f	r	o	g		
o	c	t	o	p	u	s
		g	o	o	s	e
		o	w	l		
	c	o	w			
	f	o	x			
	d	o	g			

1

2

3

4

5

6

7

8

Colour the star if you can make up
another animal puzzle of your own.